Play Learn

Sticker Activity Fun
Dinosaurs

priddy books
big ideas for little people

Picture problem

Which jigsaw piece completes the picture?

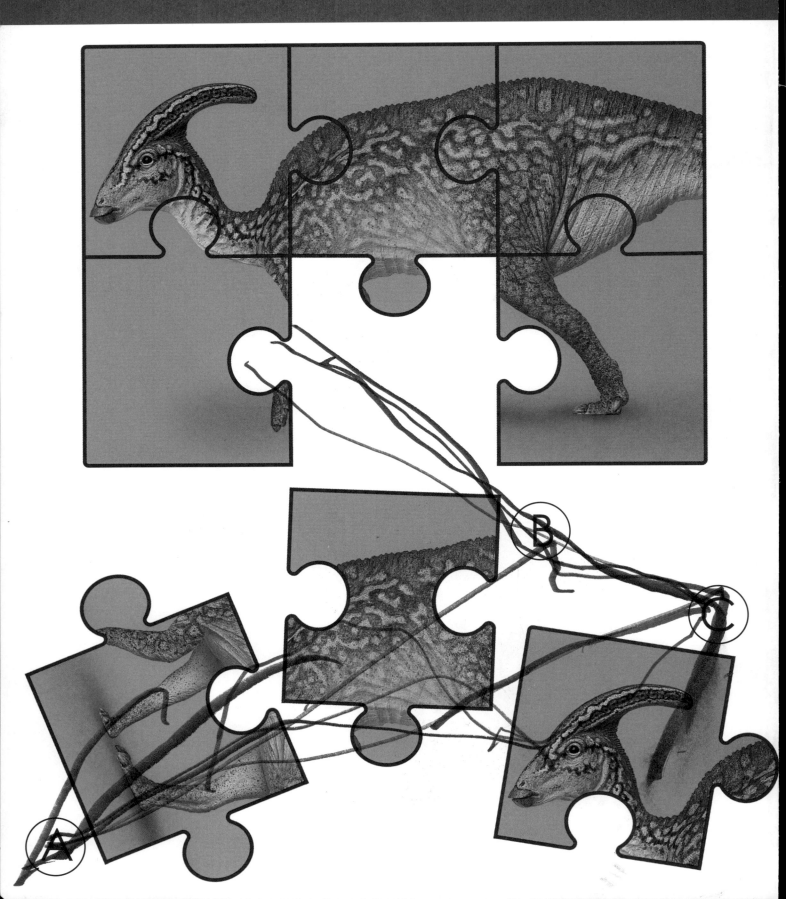

Follow the lines

Use your pen to trace over the lines between the dinosaurs.

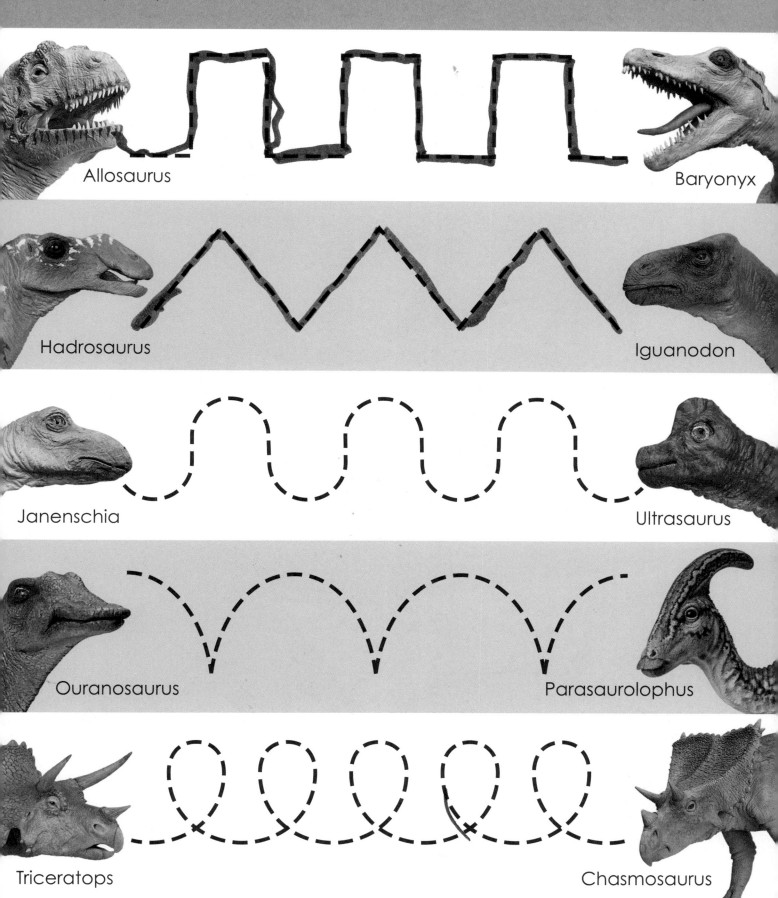

Allosaurus

Baryonyx

Hadrosaurus

Iguanodon

Janenschia

Ultrasaurus

Ouranosaurus

Parasaurolophus

Triceratops

Chasmosaurus

Counting dinosaurs

Count the dinosaurs and write the numbers of each in the boxes.

How many pictures of Diplodocus are there?

How many pictures of Coelophysis are there?

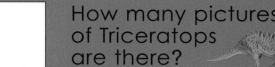

 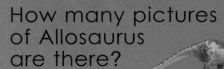

Prehistoric pictures

Find the dinosaur stickers, then color in the scenes.

1

Riojasaurus

2

Hadrosaurus

Drawing dinosaurs

Tyrannosaurus rex

Tyrannosaurus rex

look

trace

Now draw the dinosaur and write its name.

Matching letters

Draw a line between each dinosaur and the letter its name begins with.

Baryonyx

V

S

Stenonychosaurus

U

Velociraptor

B

L

Leptoceratops

Ultrasaurus

Adding dinosaurs

Write the numbers of dinosaurs in the boxes,
then add them together.

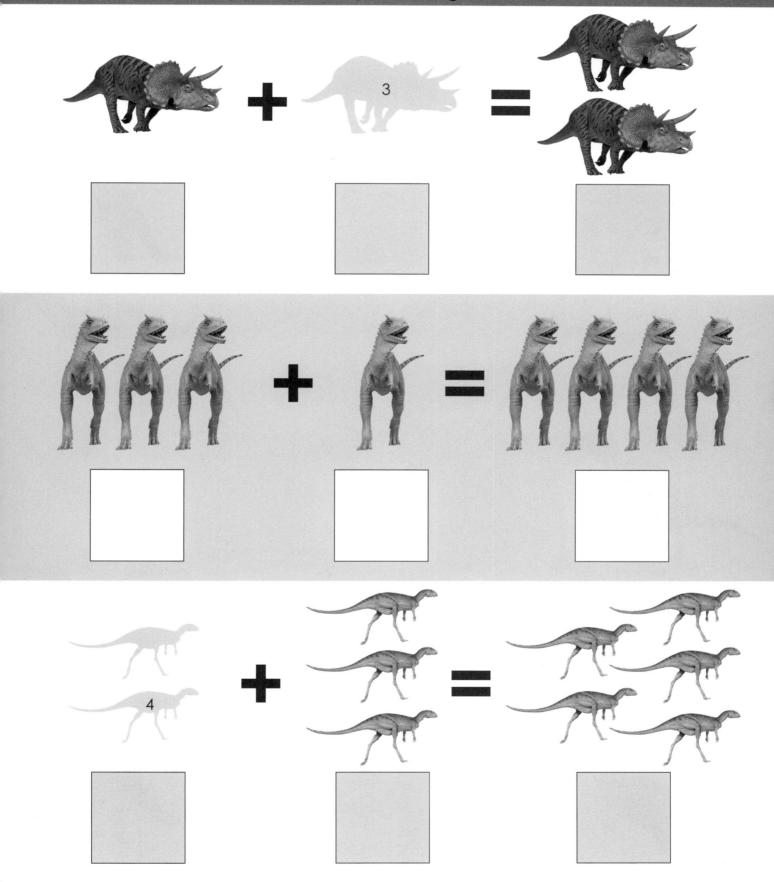

Mix and match

Draw lines between the matching pairs of dinosaurs.

What do I eat?

Carnivores eat meat and herbivores eat plants.
Circle all of the meat-eating dinosaurs.

I am a Xenotarsosaurus.
I am a carnivore.

I am a Hadrosaurus.
I am an herbivore.

I am a
Riojasaurus.
I am an
herbivore.

I am a
Tyrannosaurus rex.
I am a
carnivore.

I am a Nodosaurus.
I am an herbivore.

I am a Zephyrosaurus.
I am an herbivore.

Drawing dinosaurs

Look at the picture and the dinosaur name, then trace the outlines.

Triceratops

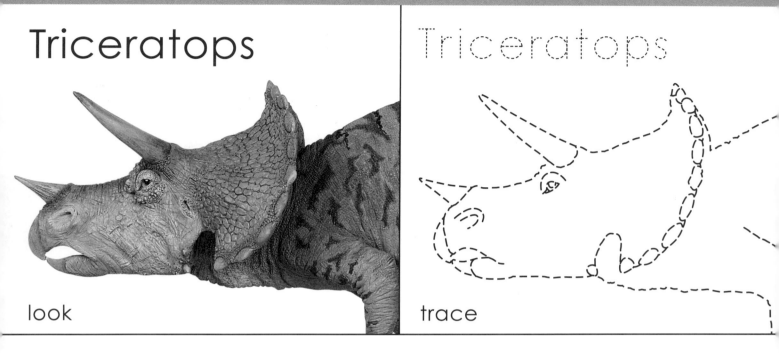

look

Triceratops

trace

Now draw the dinosaur and write its name.

T_____

How many?

Count the dinosaurs and write each number in the boxes.

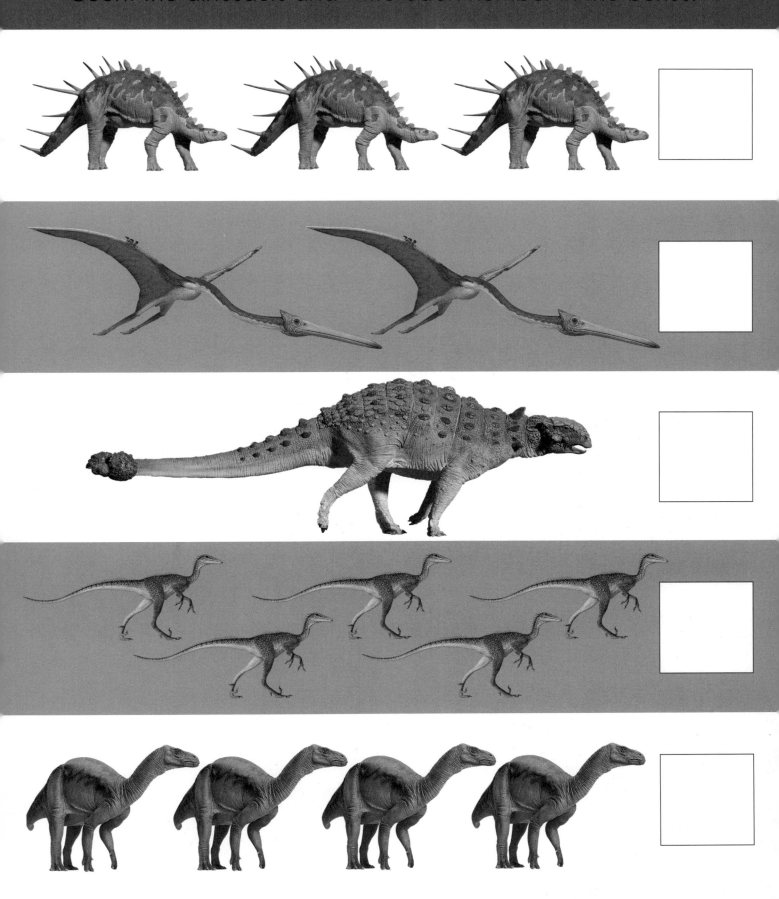

Find the stickers

Find the stickers that fit the spaces below.
Which one matches the picture?

Dot to dot

Join the dots to complete the dinosaur pictures, then color them in using the colored dots as a guide.

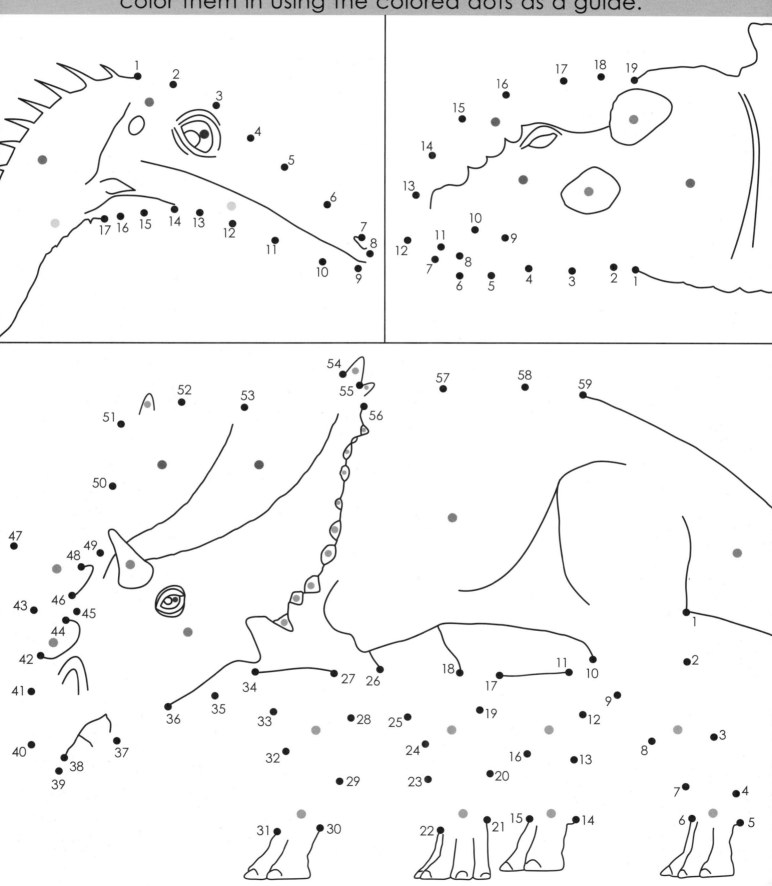

What's different?

There are six differences between these pictures.
Circle each difference on picture B when you spot them.

A

B

Dinosaur maze

Find a way through the maze so that
the dinosaur can join his friends.

start

finish

Who's missing?

Which dinosaur in picture A does not appear in picture B?

B

Drawing dinosaurs

Look at the picture and the dinosaur name, then trace the outlines.

Stegosaurus

look

Stegosaurus

trace

Now draw the dinosaur and write its name.

S_____

tail

horns

teeth

claws

What's different?

There are six differences between these two pictures.
Circle the differences on picture B when you find them.

A

B

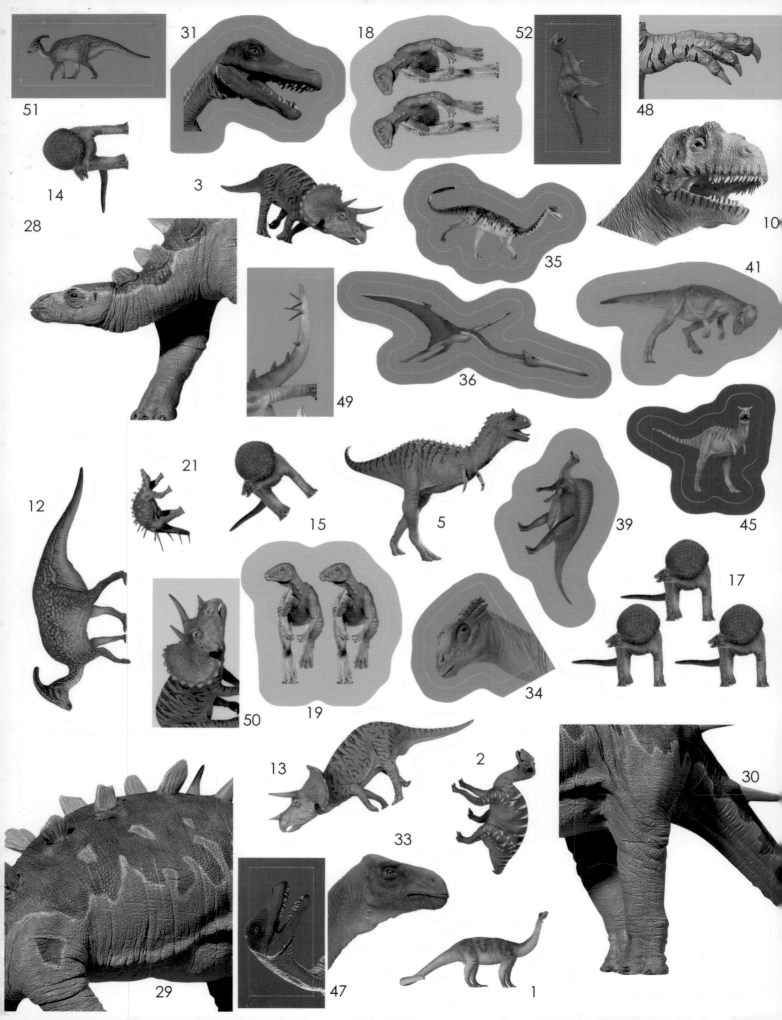

51

31

18

52

48

14

28

3

35

10

41

36

49

21

15

5

39

45

12

17

13

2

30

33

50

19

34

29

47

1

9

24

26

38

32

43

42

7

22

4

20

37

23

11

44

46

16

40

25

6

27

8

Reptile trail

Which trail will take the baby Quetzalcoatlus to its mother?

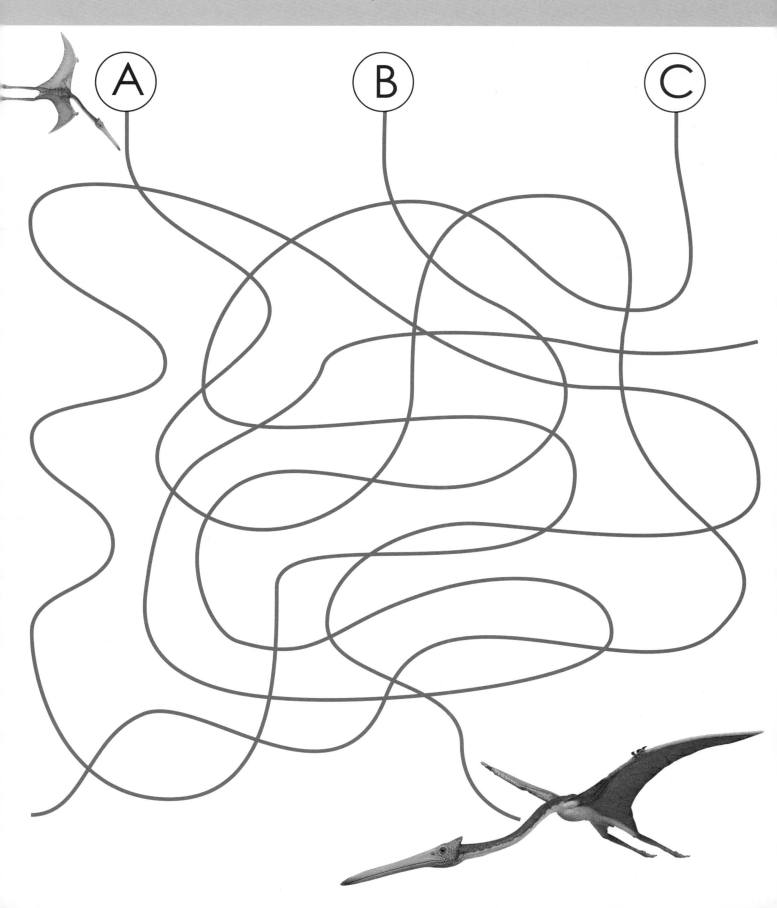

Matching pairs

Draw lines between the matching pairs of dinosaurs.

Drawing dinosaurs

Look at the picture and dinosaur name, then trace the outlines.

Fabrosaurus

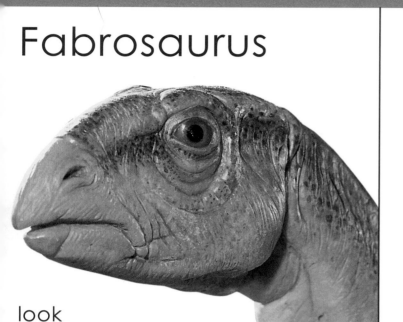

look

Fabrosaurus

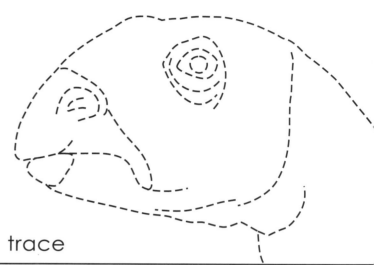

trace

Now draw the dinosaur and write its name.

F _ _ _ _ _ _ _ _ _ _

Prehistoric picture

Use your pens or pencils to color in this dinosaur scene.

Dinosaur names

Trace over the letters to write these dinosaur names.

Diplodocus

Diplodocus

Ultrasaurus

Ultrasaurus

Janenschia

Janenschia

Drawing dinosaurs

Look at the dinosaur picture and name, then trace the outlines.

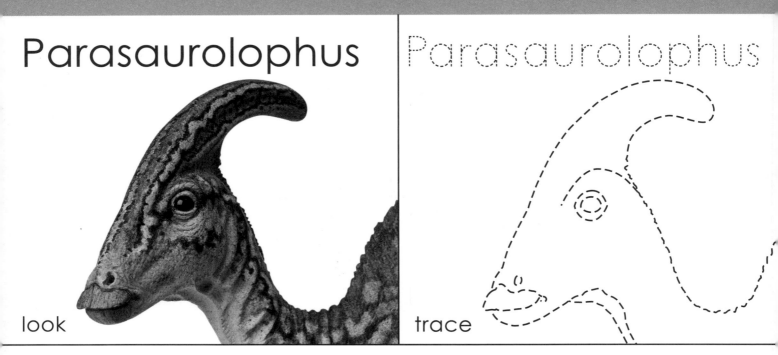

Parasaurolophus

look

Parasaurolophus

trace

Now draw the dinosaur and write its name.

P_____

Macroplata maze

Can you find a way through the maze so the
Macroplata can join his friends?

start

finish

What's different?

Which one of these creatures is different from the others?

Riojasaurus

Quetzalcoatlus

Nodosaurus

Ouranosaurus

Missing halves

Find the stickers, then draw the other halves of the dinosaurs.

Parasaurolophus

12

13

Triceratops

Adding dinosaurs

Find the stickers, write the numbers of dinosaurs in the boxes, then add them together.

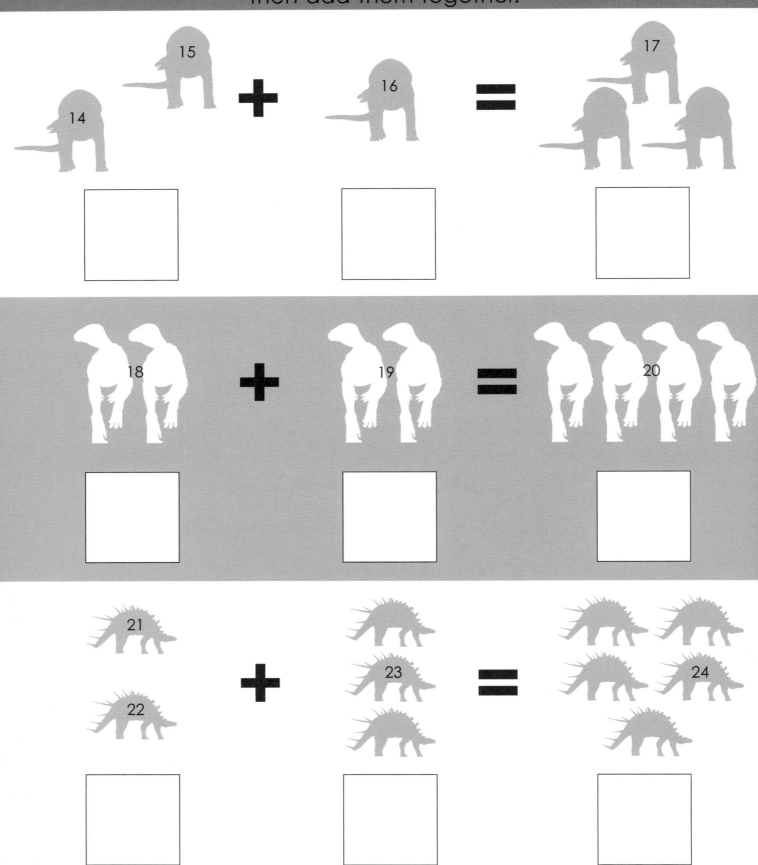

Jigsaw puzzle

Find the jigsaw stickers that complete the pictures.

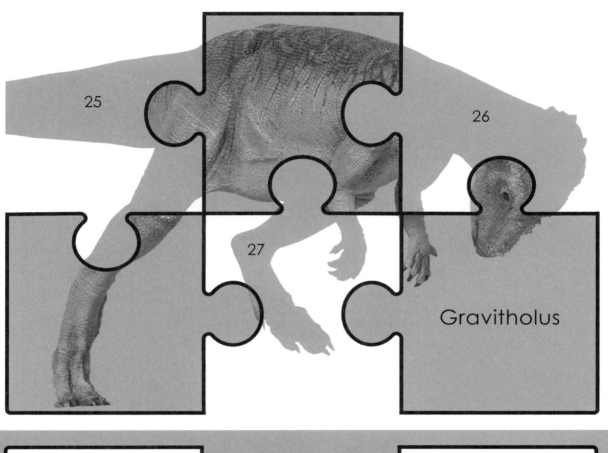

25

26

27

Gravitholus

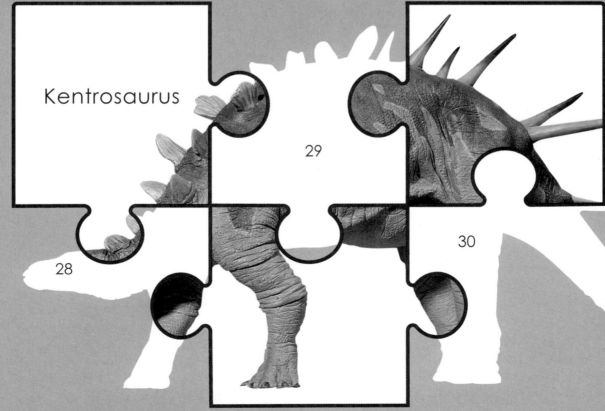

Kentrosaurus

29

28

30

Prehistoric portraits

Find the stickers, then color in the pictures that match.

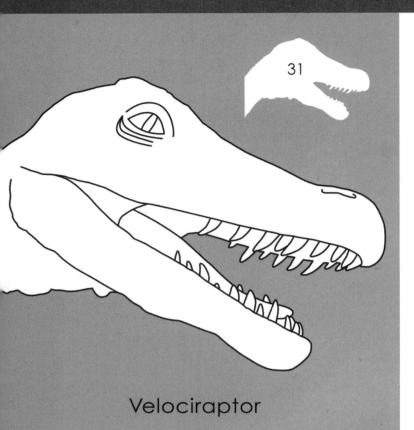

Velociraptor

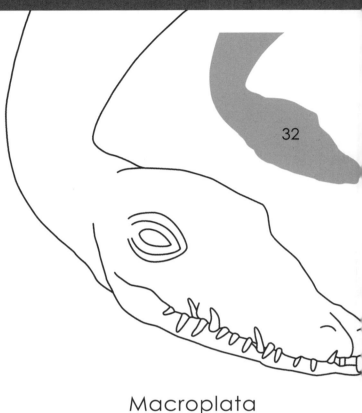

Macroplata

Iguanodon

Wannanosaurus

Writing practice

Trace over the letters of these dinosaur words.

spikes

eye

neck

tail

Dot to dot

Join the dots to complete the pictures, then color them in using the colored dots as a guide.

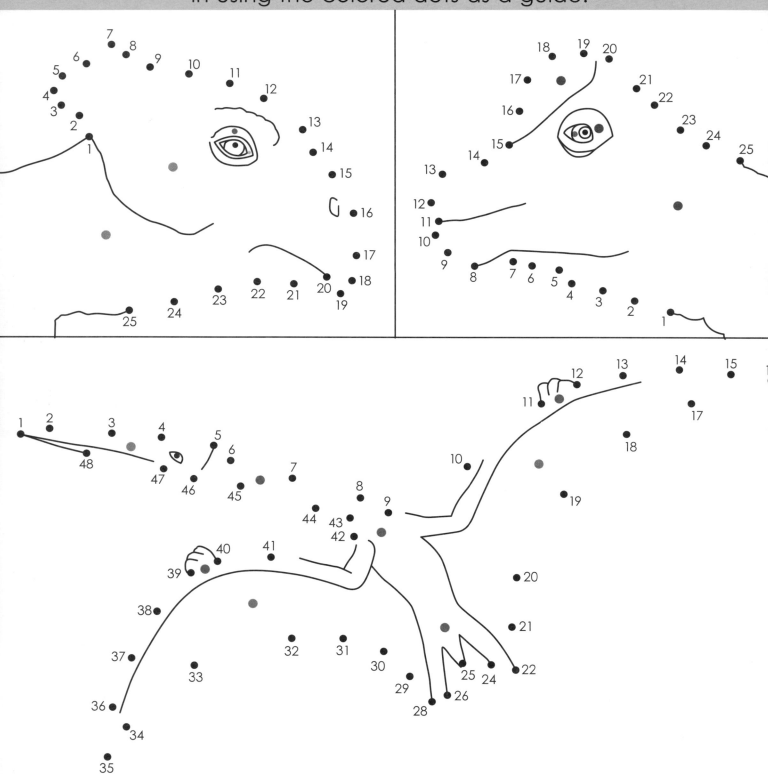

Exactly the same

Only two of these dinosaurs are exactly the same.
Look closely to find them.

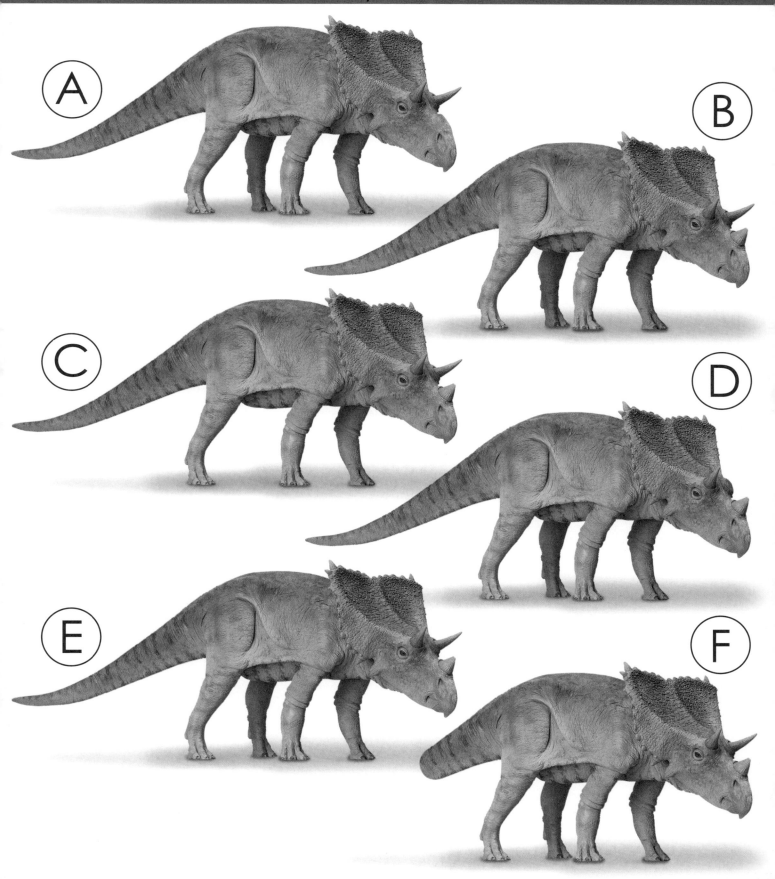

Number practice

Trace over the outlines to practice writing numbers and find the stickers that fit on the opposite page.

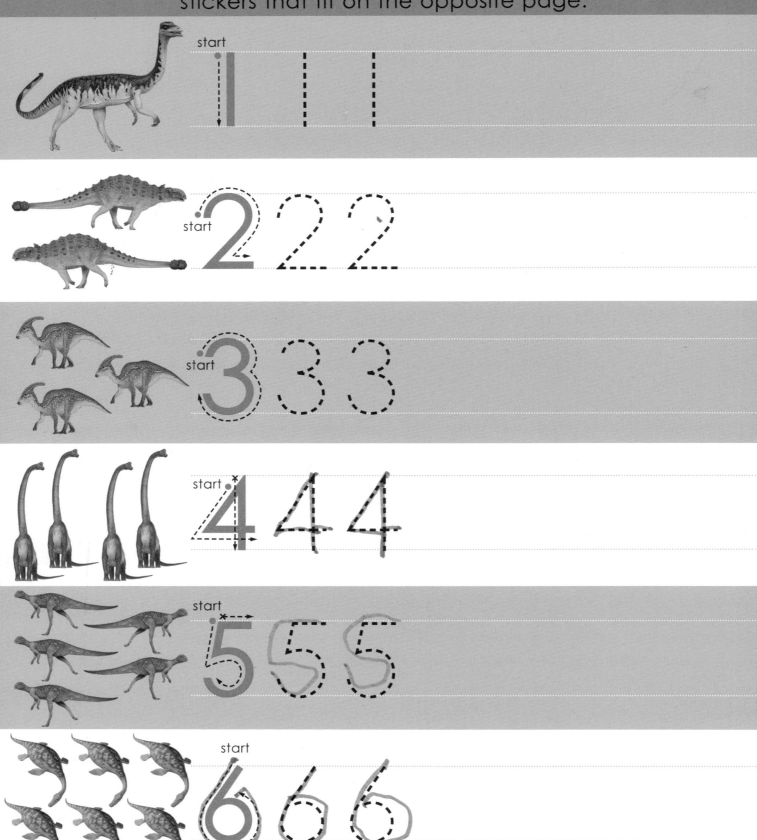

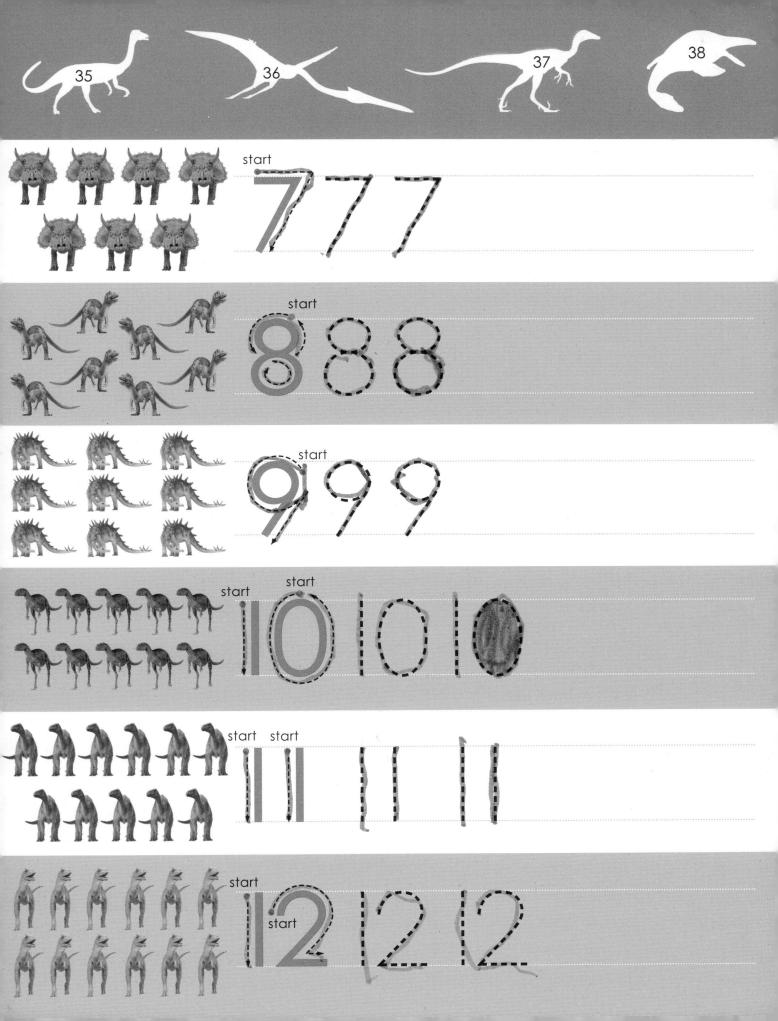

start
7 7 7

start
8 8 8

start
9 9 9

start start
10 10 10

start start
11 11 11

start
12 12 12
start

Letter practice

Trace over the outlines to practice writing letters and find the stickers that fit on the opposite page.

start
A A

start

start
B B

start

start

start

start
D D

start

start
E E

start
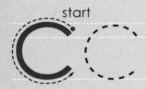

start

start
F F

start

start
G G

start
g g

start
H H

start
h h

start
I I

start
i i

start
J J

start
j j

start
K K

start
k k

start
L L

start
l l

Letter practice

Trace over the outlines to practice writing letters and find the stickers that fit on the opposite page.

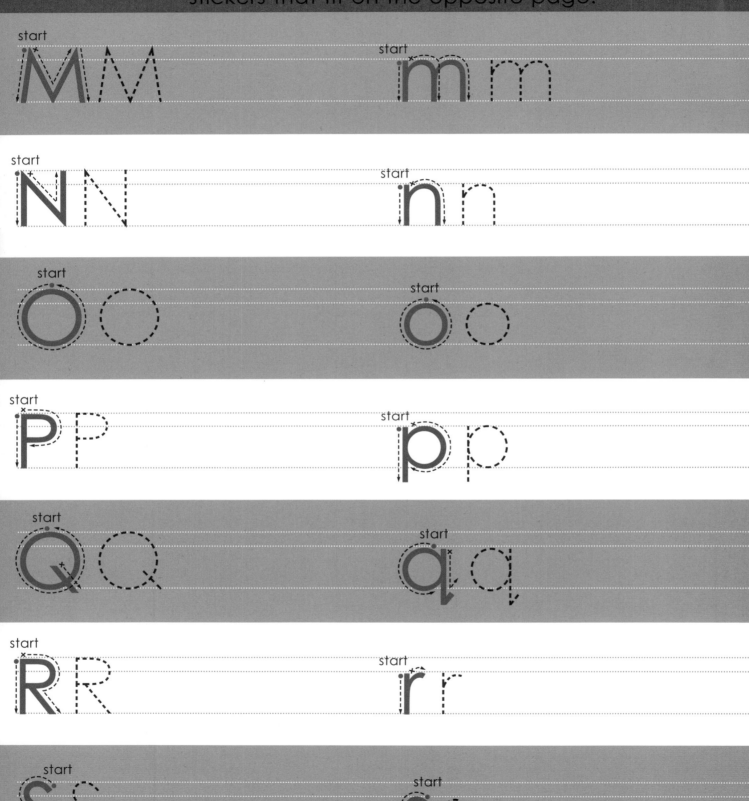

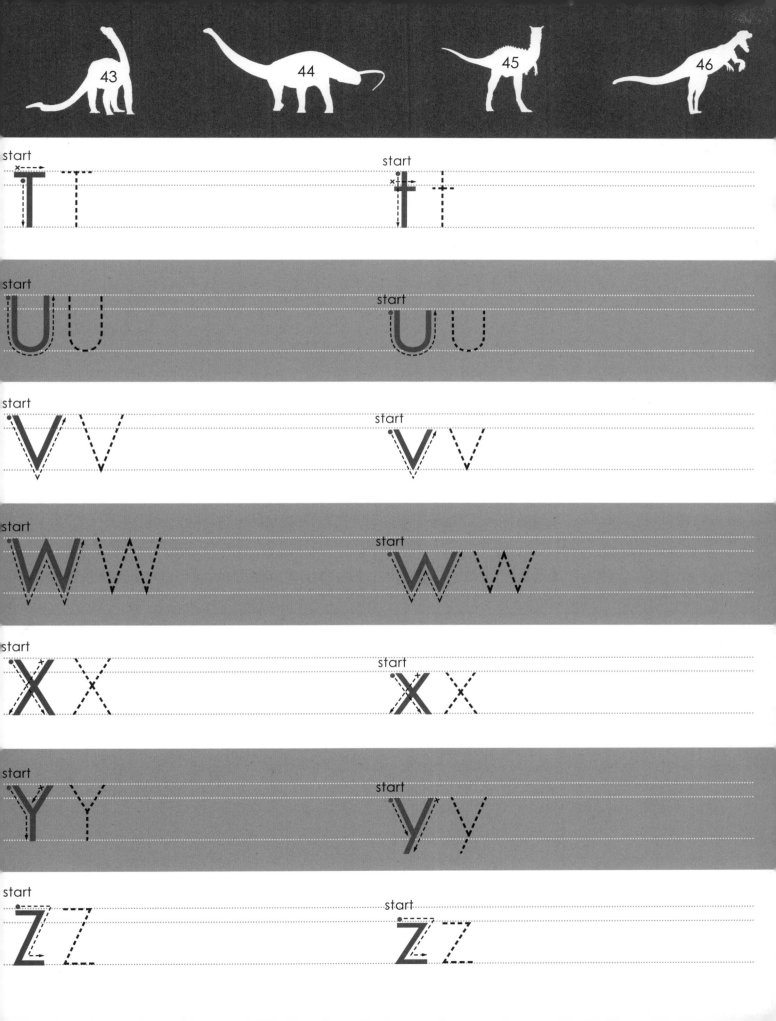

start
T T

start
T t

start
U U

start
U u

start
V V

start
V v

start
W W

start
W w

start
X X

start
X x

start
Y Y

start
Y y

start
Z Z

start
Z z

Word search

Find the stickers, then look for the words in the box.

x	d	r	y	j	t	e	r	c	o
a	y	i	d	a	a	k	t	l	p
r	e	x	n	e	i	d	i	a	a
e	h	e	a	o	l	e	z	w	s
f	w	o	i	o	s	x	s	s	w
j	i	u	r	u	e	a	i	g	e
g	a	n	h	n	m	t	u	i	t
s	a	e	x	s	s	r	v	r	r
t	e	e	t	h	u	e	n	o	e
b	c	z	s	l	i	s	a	m	x

 47 teeth

 48 claws

 49 tail

 50 horns

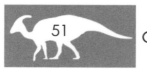 51 dinosaur

 52 T rex